Dribble, Shoot, Score!

Joe Layden

SCHOLASTIC INC.

New York   Toronto   London   Auckland   Sydney

*To Mrs. Roth's first grade class... and the rest of
the kids at Lake Avenue Elementary School
—J.L.*

Photo Credits
Cover (Left), Back cover, 9, 24: NBA/Bill Baptist. **Cover (Middle):** NBA/Richard Lewis. **Cover (Right):** NBA/ Jeff Reinking. **3, 14, 23, 30:** NBA/Andrew D. Bernstein. **17, 25:** NBA/Nathaniel S. Butler. **6:** NBA/Steve DiPaola. **7, 11, 28, 29:** NBA/Scott Cunningham. **10:** NBA/ Ron Hoskins. **4, 12, 21, 22:** NBA/Barry Gossage. **18:** NBA/Dale Tait. **26:** NBA/Ray Amati. **27:** NBA/Fernando Medina. **31:** NBA/Glenn James.

ISBN 0-590-13767-0

© 1997 by NBA Properties, Inc.
All rights reserved. Published by Scholastic Inc.

12 11 10 9 8 7 6 5 4 3 2 1   7 8 9/9 0 1 2/0

Printed in the U.S.A.
First Scholastic printing, February 1997
Book design: Gewirtz Graphics, Inc.

Welcome to a night in the National Basketball Association (NBA). Two hours of nonstop action, featuring the greatest athletes in the world. The players have finished warming up. Introductions have been made. So hang onto your seat. It's almost **show time!**

Nick Anderson is introduced before the start of the game.

Show Time

Jump Ball

Every game begins with a **jump ball**. Players from both teams gather near the center-court circle. A **referee** positions himself between two of the tallest players — one from each team. The referee tosses the ball high. The two athletes spring into action, leaping and reaching. The ball is tipped. The game is on!

Patrick Ewing and Earvin Johnson compete for the jump ball.

Dribbl

Dribbling is an essential skill used to move the ball up and down the court. In the hands of a quick and confident **point guard**, the ball almost becomes a part of the body. The ball moves as he moves, rising and falling with each step.

John Stockton, dribbling.

His touch is light, but sure. His fingers flick the ball to the floor and then wait for its return. He hears the bounce and feels for the ball. His eyes scan the court, looking for an open teammate.

Mitch Richmond, dribbling.

Defense

The defender slides over to meet the man he must cover. He tries to match the **ballhandler's** every move. The job of the **defense** is easily defined: Prevent the other team from scoring. And yet, defense is the hardest part of basketball.

The best defender is strong and quick. He has an ability to guess what his opponent will do next. The defender is sometimes overlooked by the crowd, but his hard work can mean the difference between winning and losing.

Don Reid and Grant Hill defend the basket.

The ballhandler fakes to his right. With a neat **crossover dribble** he cuts back to his left. The defender freezes, giving the offensive player an opening. The ballhandler rises for a **jump shot**. He hangs in the air, nearly motionless, suspended for just a moment.

◄ *Reggie Miller gets set...*
and goes up for the shot. ▶

Jump

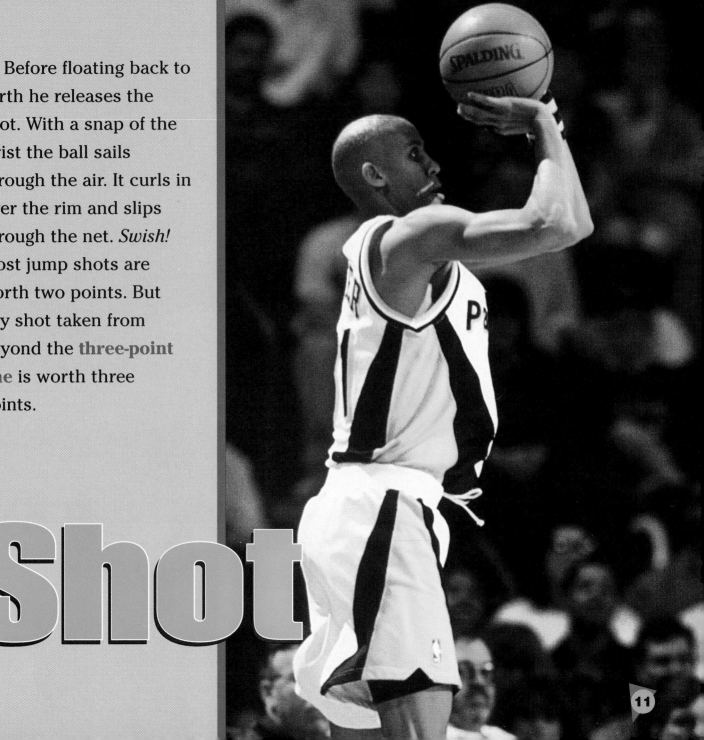

Before floating back to earth he releases the shot. With a snap of the wrist the ball sails through the air. It curls in over the rim and slips through the net. *Swish!* Most jump shots are worth two points. But any shot taken from beyond the **three-point line** is worth three points.

Shot

When a shot is released, offensive and defensive players jostle for position. They plant their feet and prepare for the **rebound**. Bodies bump. Elbows and knees become entangled.

Each player wants to hold his ground. He tries to stay between his man and the basket. This strange dance is known as **boxing out**. It is a vital part of the game. Boxing out often determines who will get the ball when a shot is missed.

Box Out

Hakeem Olajuwon boxes out Shaquille O'Neal.

Rebound

All eyes follow the flight of the ball. It rattles against the rim and bounces high into the air. On the floor, the struggle continues. Players push and lean and prepare to jump. Each hopes to **rebound** the basketball and take possession for his team.

Dennis Rodman and Magic Johnson battle for the rebound.

Block

The rebound is controlled by a player on the offensive team. He decides to take another shot. The action moves quickly. He dribbles once... twice. Defenders converge on the shooter as he moves toward the basket and releases the ball.

One defender leaps high. He reaches out and swats the ball away. The crowd roars!

A **blocked shot** is one of the most impressive plays in basketball.

Five-foot seven-inch Spud Webb
leaps high to block a shot.

Fast

The force of the blocked shot carries the ball out past the three-point line. Players scramble to retrieve it. Suddenly, the defense becomes the offense. The game changes direction.

Break

A smaller player dribbles down the middle of the floor at full speed. One teammate sprints to his left, another to his right. The ballhandler looks ahead. The **fast break** begins.

Muggsy Bogues leads the fast break.

No-Look Pass

The best way to stop a fast break is to wait for the offense to reveal its plan of attack. The defenders move into position. They look for a signal.

There it is! The ballhandler glances to his left. The defenders lean in that direction, hoping to intercept the pass. But it's a trick. In one fluid motion the ballhandler picks up his dribble and snaps off a crisp, **no-look pass** to a teammate on his right. The defense has gambled . . . and lost.

Allan Houston looks one way . . .
and passes another.

Layup

The fast break often ends with a **layup**. A player receives a pass near the three-point line. With a clear path to the basket, he simply dribbles in, jumps, and lets the ball roll off his fingertips. It kisses the glass and slides through the hoop.

◀ *Mookie Blaylock goes in for the easy layup.*

Magic Johnson passes to a teammate.

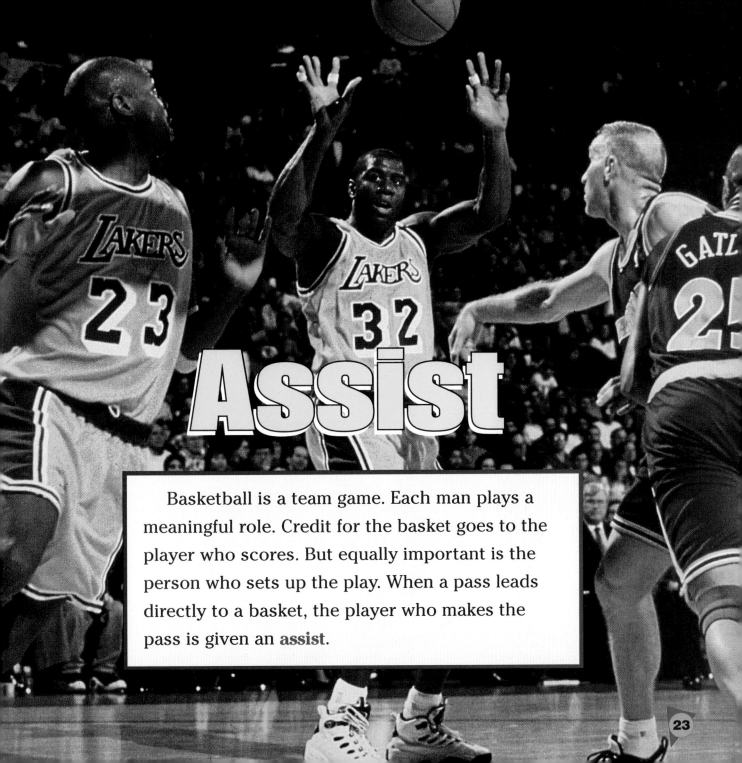

Assist

Basketball is a team game. Each man plays a meaningful role. Credit for the basket goes to the player who scores. But equally important is the person who sets up the play. When a pass leads directly to a basket, the player who makes the pass is given an **assist**.

Foul

As the offensive player shoots the ball, he is hit on the arm by a defender. The game is interrupted by the referee's whistle. Basketball is a physical sport. But when the contact is too severe, the referee will call a **foul**.

Kenny Gattison fouls David Robinson.

Sometimes, when a player is fouled, he is awarded a **free throw**. He shoots from the **foul line** while the other players watch. No one is allowed to guard a player when he is shooting a free throw. Each free throw is worth one point.

Free Throw

David Robinson at the foul line.

Horace Grant calls time-out.

Time-out

When a team wants to discuss strategy, it will ask the referee for a **time-out**. The game comes to a halt as players walk to the bench and gather around their coach. They sip water. They wipe the sweat from their hands. And they listen.

The coach points out mistakes. He offers advice and encouragement. When the buzzer sounds, signaling the end of the time-out, the players break from their huddle and return to the court. They are rested and ready.

Miami Heat coach, Pat Riley.

Steal

The ball is put into play. The defense applies heavy pressure. The point guard dribbles across the court.

The defender shadows him, matching every stride. Suddenly, he tries for the **steal**. He reaches out and pokes the ball away. The point guard stumbles. The ball is loose. The defender scoops it up.

◀ *Toni Kukoc steals the ball...*

and races upcourt. ▶

The steal leads to another fast break. The ballhandler passes ahead to a teammate, who dribbles toward the basket, a step ahead of his opponent. He rises effortlessly and **dunks** the ball through the rim!

Michael Jordan takes to the air.

am Dunk

The crowd stands and cheers. Nothing electrifies an arena quite like a slam dunk. It energizes team-mates, discourages opponents, and thrills fans. A slam dunk always brings fans to their feet.

The dunk is one of many reasons why fans love the game of basketball!

Glossary

Assist:

When a player makes a pass that leads directly to a basket by a teammate, it is called an assist.

Ballhandler:

The offensive player who controls the basketball is known as the ballhandler.

Block:

When a defender uses his hand to swat away an opponent's shot, it is called a block.

Boxing out:

When a shot is taken, a player who tries to stay between his man and the basket is boxing out. By boxing out the opponent, a player gets in position to rebound the basketball.

Crossover dribble:

When a player switches the ball from one hand to the other by bouncing it in front of his body, it is called a crossover dribble.

Defense:

The team that does not have possession of the ball is the defense. The goal of the defense is to prevent the offense from scoring.

Dribbling:

When a player taps the ball with his hand so that it bounces one or more times on the floor, it is known as dribbling. Dribbling is the most common way for a player to control the ball.

Dunk:

A dunk occurs when a player scores by throwing the ball through the rim with force. The dunk is one of the most exciting plays in basketball.

Fast break:

A fast break occurs when one team suddenly gains possession of the ball and tries to score by sprinting quickly down the court. The defense is often outnumbered on a fast break.

Foul:

When a player holds, pushes, or charges into an opponent, he is called for a foul.

Foul line:

The foul line is 15 feet from the backboard. When a player attempts a free throw, he shoots from the foul line.

Free throw:

A free throw is a shot that is awarded to a player after a foul has been committed. Each free throw is worth one point.

Jump ball:

A jump ball is one way in which the referee determines which team will have possession of the ball. One player from each team stands in the jump circle. The referee tosses the ball in the air. Each player tries to tap the ball to a teammate. Every game begins with a jump ball.

Jump shot:

When an offensive player leaps in the air and shoots the ball from outside, it is called a jump shot.

Layup:

A layup is one of the safest shots in basketball. A player drives to the basket, jumps, and lays the ball in from only a few inches away.

No-look pass:

When a player looks in one direction while passing the ball in another direction, he is making a no-look pass.

Point guard:

The point guard is usually the best dribbler on the team. He brings the ball down the court and directs the offense.

Rebound:

When a player grabs the ball out of the air after a missed shot, he is credited with a rebound.

Referee:

An official who makes sure that the rules of the game are not broken is known as a referee. The referee uses a whistle to call fouls and stop play.

Show time:

When an exciting, entertaining event is about to begin, it is known as show time. This event might be a movie, a play, or a basketball game.

Steal:

A steal occurs when a defender takes the ball away from an offensive player.

Three-point line:

The arc that stretches from one side of the floor to the other, 22 feet from the basket, is the three-point line. Any shot taken from beyond this line is worth three points.

Time-out:

When a team wants to discuss strategy with its coach, it will stop the game by asking the referee for a time-out.